The Basics of
Blackjack

J. Edward Allen

The Basics of Gambling Series
published by
Gambling Research Institute

First Printing   *October 1984*
Second Printing   *February 1985*

ISBN: 0-9607618-2-9

Book Design and Production—Santa Cruz Typesetting
Cover Design—Lois Stanfield

The GRI series is distributed by:
Cardoza Publishing
P.O. Box 5267
Santa Cruz, California 95063

Table of Contents

Illustrations & Charts

Illustrations

Charts

I. Introduction

Blackjack's popularity continues to grow, and it is by far the most popular of the table games the casino offers. The reason for this is simple: it's the only game in the house where the player can have an edge over the house.

In order to have this edge, the player must know basic strategy and play this strategy correctly. But that's not difficult to do, and it's all here in this guide—everything the player must know to play at his best and to beat the house.

The strategies shown in this book are based upon computer studies and should be studied carefully. They're explained so that anyone, after a few hours or less of practice, can be a winner at blackjack.

The book is written in simple and clear language, and its one purpose is in making you, the reader, a winner at this most popular and exciting casino game.

II. The Blackjack Scene

The area devoted to blackjack in any casino will usually be the largest area devoted to any of the table games, which include not only blackjack, but craps, roulette and baccarat. In fact, in many casinos the game is so popular that several areas may offer the game of blackjack.

It's therefore not hard to find a game when entering the casino. There will be a number of tables placed so that they surround a center area from which the casino personnel operate. This is known as the **blackjack pit**.

The Table

The blackjack table is a modified oval, with the seats arranged around the curved portion. There will be as many seats available as spots on the table.

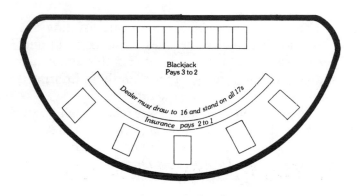

The number of seats available at a blackjack table ranges from five to seven depending upon the casino. While the players remain seated throughout the game (unless they wish to stand) the dealer stands and faces them from the inside of the pit.

Directly in front of the dealer is the chip rack, containing the casino chips. To his right (sometimes to his left) is a slot where cash is dropped when players come to the table and change cash for chips.

Also on the table may be a **shoe** which is a rectangular box, either made of plastic or wood, which holds at least four decks of cards. If the game is played with only one or two decks, there will be no shoe on the table.

There may also be a small sign stating the minimum bet (and sometimes the maximum one) permitted at the table. Sometimes this small sign shows additional rules, other than those imprinted on the green felt covering the table.

The green felt contains boxes where each player will place his chips for betting purposes, and where usually two or three rules of the game are printed. The most common is *Dealer Must Draw to 16, and Stand on All 17s*, which refers to the totals of the points the dealer holds. The next most common rule is *Insurance Pays 2-1*. The third is *Blackjack Pays 3-2*.

These are very basic rules that we need not concern ourselves with right now, for they will be fully explained at the appropriate time.

The Dealer

Unlike the players, the dealer stands throughout the game, and wears the house uniform. In these days of tighter security, there is usually some name tag and sometimes a picture of the dealer attached, so that the players can, by looking closely, ascertain the name of the dealer.

The dealer runs the game. He changes cash into chips issued by the casino; he **changes color**—that is, changing casino chips into smaller or larger denominations. He shuffles the cards, and deals them

8

out. He pays off winning bets and collects losing bets. He answers questions of the players, and is there to help them, as well as run the game.

Tipping the Dealer

Tipping, or **toking** the dealer, to use a casino term, is not required, but is often done. Some players overtip; others never tip at all. And some, if they tip, don't do it correctly.

A dealer should be toked if you feel that he or she has been friendly and helpful, and has made your game more enjoyable. In that case, every now and then you can make a bet for the dealer by putting out a chip above your box in the area marked for insurance bets.

When you do this, if you win your bet, the dealer will win his; if you lose, the dealer will also lose. The dealers prefer this kind of toking, for it gives them the chance to double the original bet, and sometimes win even more if the player is dealt a blackjack.

Sometimes players tip after a blackjack is dealt to them, but one must remember that no matter how generous you want to be, your edge at blackjack is very slight, and overtipping will erode your winnings. Strike a happy balance, but under no circumstances tip a hostile or unfriendly dealer, or one who wants you to lose and considers you a sucker for playing.

The Casino Chips

Casino personnel call chips **checks**, but we're going to use the term chips throughout this book because it's the most popular term, understood by all players.

9

These are issued by a casino in standard denominations; usually for $1, $5, $25, and $100. Some casinos have $500 and even higher denomination chips, and many casinos have 50¢ chips at the blackjack table, because payoffs are often in this amount. There are casinos that don't bother issuing chips this small, and instead pay off with coins, either half-dollars or quarters.   In some of the Northern Nevada casinos, $2.50 chips are used at the blackjack tables, saving the dealers time and trouble when payoffs for $5 blackjacks are made. A blackjack, which will be explained later, pays 3-2, and a $5 wager will be paid off with $7.50.

Players can also play with cash, but casino executives frown on this. Some players like to play only in cash, but if they win they'll have to settle for casino chips as their payoff. Dealers will always pay off in casino chips, not in cash.

Casinos have minimum betting limits, which usually are $1 or $2. Some tables may have $5 or $25 or even higher minimum limits, because *high rollers* don't want to be betting thousands while some other player is betting $2 at a time.

After you leave a table, you can cash in your casino chips at the **cashier's cage** of the casino. If you don't spot it, any security guard or other casino personnel will show you where it is. That's where you get cash for your chips, not at the blackjack table.

The Players

Even though there may be five to seven spots open for players at any blackjack table, the game will begin if one player shows up to play. When more than one player is at a table, additional players can take any of the vacant seats. There is no set rule where one is to sit.

The cards are dealt, as we shall see, in a clockwise fashion so that the player to the dealer's left, facing him, is the first player to receive cards. He is known as the **first baseman**. The player at the other end of the table, nearest to the dealer's right, is the last player to receive cards, and he's known as the **third baseman** or **anchorman.**

Where should one sit at a table if given the choice? Most experts prefer either the third baseman's seat or the one to its right, for they get a look at the other hands before they have to make any playing decisions.

But if you're a beginner, don't sit in the third baseman's seat. You might feel too much pressure, for sometimes when you draw a card you'll inadvertently make the dealer a winner. Even though you made the right decision, ignorant players may unfairly blame you for their losses. But, as you get more expert, sit as close to the third baseman's seat as you can, for you get that little extra information playing last.

Players in casino blackjack play their hands as individuals, trying to beat the dealer, not each other. When you are dealt cards, all you want to do is get a better hand than the dealer, so you can win. The other hands are immaterial to this result, and often some players at the table will win a hand while others will be losing their hands.

III. The Cards and Rules of Play

The Cards

A standard deck of 52 cards is used in the game of casino blackjack. At one time most games were played with this single deck of cards, but today there are many multiple deck games in existence. But no matter how many decks are used, whether two or eight, they are merely multiples of the standard 52 deck game. Therefore, if a player is at a table where two decks are used, the dealer is using 104 cards, made up of two standard decks of 52 cards each.

The standard deck of cards contains four suits; clubs, diamonds, hearts and spades. In blackjack, the suits have no material value and can be disregarded. What is important is the value of the cards.

Value of the Cards

Each of the four suits contains the identical 13

cards, ranging from an ace to a king. The cards are ace, 2, 3, 4, 5, 6, 7, 8, 9, 10, jack, queen and king.

In casino blackjack, the following cards are counted as 10s, and have that value for adding purposes to ascertain the total of the hand: 10, jack, queen and king.

In the future, we'll refer to any of these cards as a **10-value card** or simply as a **10.** There are sixteen 10-value cards in the standard deck, and therefore these are the most frequent cards in play. All the other values consist of only four cards.

To value a card, other than the ace, which we'll write about last, we simply examine the spots on the card, as well as the numerical value in the form of a number at the corners. Thus a 2 has two spots, the 3 three, the 4 four, and all the way up to the 9, which has 9 spots.

The ace is the most powerful card in blackjack, and one of the reasons for its importance is that it can be valued, at the option of the player, as either a 1 or 11.

Blackjack is also called **21** because that is the highest total that a player may validly hold. Any hand totaling more than 21 points is a loser, and so called a **"bust."** The ace, which can be valued at 1 or 11, sometimes prevents hands from going over 21, or "busting"—that is, losing, when it is valued as a 1.

For example, a hand containing 10-3-ace is merely a 14, not a 24, because the player simply values the ace as a 1. The ace gives players, especially beginners, the most trouble. Often they think they've busted, or lost, because they value the ace as an 11 instead of as a 1. If in doubt, show the hand to the dealer and let him value it for you.

Object of the Game

When we discuss the object of the game, we write about the object from the player's standpoint. The dealer has no object to his play; he simply must follow the rules set forth by the casino, which is to stand on hands of 17 or more, and draw to all hands of 16 or less.

The object of the game, in its most simple terms, is to beat the dealer. To do this, the player can win in two ways. First of all, he or she must have a total higher than the dealer's total, or he or she must have a valid hand, of whatever total, while the dealer "busts" or goes over 21.

The player loses if his or her total is less than the dealer's total, or if the player busts. Once the player busts, his hand is out of play and his bet is removed. It doesn't matter to this player if the dealer subsequently busts his own hand; once the player busts, he loses.

If both the player and the dealer have the same totals in their respective hands, it's a tie, a standoff. The casino term for this is a **"push."** And that's just what it is, a push. Neither the player nor the dealer win.

How does a player improve his total? First, to understand this concept, we have to look at the original hand dealt to the player.

The Original Hand

The dealer, to put a round of play in motion, deals out two cards to each of the players and two cards to himself. The cards are dealt one at a time, face down, the player to the dealer's left getting the first card, and then each player after that getting a card in clockwise fashion. After each player has received one card, then the dealer gives himself a card, also face down. Then a second card is dealt to each of the players, also face down, in the same order, and the dealer gets his second card, and turns it face up.

This face up card is known as the **upcard**. Thus, all the players see one of the dealer's cards, but the dealer sees none of the players' cards. It wouldn't matter if he saw the players' cards or not, for the dealer, as we have said, is bound by strict rules. In some casinos, in multiple deck games, the players' cards are dealt face up.

Most players prefer to have their cards dealt face down, for it gives them a feeling they're actually involved in a secret game of some sort, hiding their cards from the dealer, who couldn't care less. But most experts prefer to see all the cards dealt face up, because they get a better grasp of what cards are in play and out of the deck, and this gives them a slight advantage.

The two cards the player gets at the outset of play is an original hand. The highest total he can get is 21 on on original hand; an ace and a 10-value card. When a player (or dealer) gets this hand, it's known as a **blackjack**, or a **natural**. A blackjack pays 3-2 if it wins. All other winning hands pay even-money. If a dealer gets a blackjack and none of the players have a blackjack, the dealer simply wins the player's bet at even-money; he doesn't get that extra bonus.

If a player and the dealer have a blackjack, then it's a push; neither win.

The next highest total is a 20. This is a very strong hand, and usually a winning one, either on the part of the dealer or the player. Thereafter, the hands go down in value.

The important thing to remember is that neither a player nor a dealer can bust on the original hand. The following are some original hands and their totals:

Hand	Total
queen-5	15
9-8	17
4-8	12
10-king	20
ace-8	19

Hitting and Standing

If a player wants to improve his hand, he can draw a card to that hand. This is called **hitting** or **drawing**. For example, if a player is dealt a 5-3, his total is only 8. Even if he hits the hand, he can't bust, or go over 21. So he hits the hand, not worrying about busting.

If a player is dealt a 10-king, he has a total of 20. He doesn't want to hit this hand, for his total is very strong, just one below the highest possible total, and if he hits the hand he will bust unless he gets an ace, and the odds against getting one of the four aces is very high indeed, so he stands.

Hard and Soft Totals

Any hand that doesn't contain an ace is a **hard** hand, and the total of those hard hands are **hard totals**. Most of the hands dealt to either the player or the dealer will be hard hands like these.

Some examples of hard hands:

5-4, which is a hard 9.
10-5, which is a hard 15.
Jack-king, which is a hard 20.

There is another way to have a hard hand, and that is to have a hand containing an ace, where the ace is counted as 1, not as an 11. For example, suppose the player were dealt an original hand of 10-4, and hit it and got an ace. He now would have hard 15, because he must value the ace as 1. If he valued it as an 11, the hand would total 25 and bust.

Other hard hands containing an ace:

10-6-ace, which is a hard 17.
9-4-ace, which is a hard 14.
8-3-ace, which is a hard 12.

Any hand which contains an ace that is valued at 11, rather than as 1, is a **soft** hand, and its total is a **soft total.**

For example, suppose a player received an original hand of ace-9. It would be a soft 20, with the ace counted as an 11. Of course, the player would have the option of counting the hand a 10, but that would be foolish, since his 20 is very strong, and if he counted it as a 10 and hit the hand, any card drawn other than an ace or ten-value would weaken the hand.

Here are some examples of soft hands:
ace-9 is a soft 20.
ace-8 is a soft 19.
ace-7 is a soft 18.

A soft hand has one important advantage. Even if the hand is hit, it can't bust. So if a foolish player hit a soft 20, consisting of an ace and 9, he still coudn't bust.

A soft hand can become a hard hand, if it's drawn to. For example, if a player were dealt an ace-6 for a soft 17 and hit and got an 8, his hand would now be a hard 15 (ace-6-8 = 15). An ace-4, which is a soft 15, if hit with a 7, would become a hard 12. But the same ace-4, if hit with a 5, would become a soft 20.

We'll go into the strategies of hitting or standing on soft totals later on.

The Blackjack

This is the strongest of all hands, and consists of an ace and a 10-value card (10, jack, queen or king) dealt as an original hand. It is an immediate winner for the player—unless the dealer has a blackjack also, in which case it is a push. But if the dealer doesn't have a blackjack, it pays off at 3-2.

If the dealer has a blackjack and none of the players have one, then the dealer wins all the bets at the table.

As we shall see, the player has an option of splitting aces and playing each ace as a separate hand. If a ten-value card is dealt to a split ace, it's not a blackjack, just a 21.

Remember, only an ace and a 10-value card in the original hand is a blackjack.

Busting

Sometimes this is also known as **breaking**, but busting is the more common term used in casinos. When either a player or a dealer has drawn cards to his or her original hand and gone over 21, the hand is a losing one; for he or she has busted. The only valid hands are those of 21 or fewer points.

When we bust—that is, go over 21 after hitting our hand—we must turn the cards over immediately to show that we lost, and the dealer will, at that point, take away both our cards and our chips. We've lost, and are out of the game for that round of play, even if the dealer subsequently busts. This is the really big edge the casino has over us. If the dealer and the player both bust, the player still loses.

Well, then, you might ask, why would anyone risk drawing and busting a hand? As we shall see, there are times when the dealer's upcard forces us to hit our hand, even though we may bust, because he probably has a 17 or higher total, and if we stand with a **stiff** total, or 12 to 16, we'll lose our bets without even trying to improve our hands.

IV. Playing the Casino Game

We're now ready to see how the game is played in a casino. For purposes of this illustration, we're going to assume we enter a casino to play some 21. The first thing we do is head for the blackjack pit, and look for a table that will accommodate our wagers. If we wish to bet only $2 a hand, we must find a table with a $1 or $2 minimum, and avoid the tables with a $5 or higher minimum.

We find several tables like that, and at one table only two other players are seated, one in the first baseman's spot at the extreme left of the dealer. The other player is in the center spot, so we move to the anchorman's seat and take out some cash, place it on the table, and wait for the dealer to change this into casino chips.

The dealer is about to shuffle up the cards, and so he puts them down and takes our cash. Our involvement with casino blackjack is about to begin.

Changing Cash into Chips

We are already seated in the last chair when the dealer takes our cash and counts it. We had put down $40, in assorted $10s and $20s, and the dealer will turn the money over after counting it, to verify that it's not *funny money* with one denomination printed on the front and a different one printed on the back.

In most casinos, he'll not only verify the amount with us by announcing *forty dollars*, but will try and catch the attention of a casino executive, a floorman, who will be in the interior of the pit, supervising the games. After the floorman acknowledges that this cash amount is being exchanged for chips, the dealer will drop the cash into a slot and it will disappear from view.

Then he'll give us $40 worth of chips. Since it's a $2 table, he might give us $20 worth of $1 chips and four $5 chips. We count the chips after he gives them to us. Anyone can make a mistake, and this is perfectly acceptable behavior.

While we're doing this, the dealer is shuffling the cards.

Shuffling, Cutting and Burning a Card

In the casino we're playing at, there are both one-deck and multiple-deck games, but we've sat at a table with a one-deck game. The dealer is shuffling up the cards, doing a thorough job. When he's finished, the cards are placed on the table in front of one of the players to be cut. Some players, out of superstition, refuse to cut the cards, which is also acceptable. But the player sitting in the first base cuts them by taking up a portion of the cards and placing them next to the original stack of cards. In some casinos, a plastic card is handed to the player to be inserted somewhere in the deck, then the cards on top of the card are placed below it. Either cut is legitimate.

After the cards are cut, the dealer places them all together, and then removes the top card, and either places it on the bottom of the deck, face up (but in such a manner that the players cannot see its value) or takes the top card and places it in a small plastic case to his right, face down. If he does the latter, then all future discards—that is, cards already played out—will be placed atop that card. If he turns the card face up at the bottom of the deck, then all future discards will be placed face up below that burned card.

The above paragraph describes what is meant by **burning a card**. This is a ritual carried out in practically all casinos, and hearkens back to the days when the casino was worried that someone would cut to a precise part of the deck, and thus take advantage of knowledge of the top card. Which still might be done, for all we know.

Making a Bet

As the dealer holds the cards, getting ready to deal, the players make their bets. We will see a rectangular printed box right in front of our seat, and this is where our chips go.

The bet must be made prior to the deal of the cards. It must be at least the minimum allowed at the table, and cannot be more than the maximum permitted at the table.

But we're not thinking of $500 bets (usually the maximum at most casinos) as we put out two $1 chips. We're going to get our feet wet and test the waters that Lady Luck swims in so cunningly. Our chips are now in our betting box, and since the other two players have also made their bets, the dealer is ready to deal out the cards.

The Deal

The first baseman gets the top card, face down, and then the second player gets his card, and we then get ours. The last of the first cards to be dealt goes to the dealer, also face down. Now a second card goes out in the same order, but the dealer turns over this card, his upcard.

We now all have original hands of two cards, and can exercise our various options, or *act upon* our hands. For purposes of this illustration, we're simply going to make a decision as to whether to hit or stand.

Hitting or Standing—How To

To refresh our recollection, hitting means drawing a card to our original hand. We can hit our hand as often as we care to, so long as the total of the cards doesn't exceed 21.

To hit—that is, ask for another card—we pick up our original cards and scrape the edges on the felt surface toward us. This is the universal signal for a hit in all casinos that deal cards face down. The dealer will give you another card from the top of the stock he's holding in his hand.

If we want another card after our original hit, we scrape again. Simple as that. If we're satisfied with our hand, we slide the cards under our bet chips, and don't touch either the cards or the chips again.

As you may have noticed, no verbal commands are given to the dealer. The whole game can be played silently with these signals.

Single Deck

Hitting

Standing

Hitting and Standing in Multiple Deck Games

When all the players' cards are dealt *face up*, which is the usual case in multiple deck games involving four or more decks, there are different signals used by players when they wish to hit or stand.

If a player wants to draw another card, his signal for a hit is to point his index finger at the cards. Another card will be given to him by the dealer. Or the player may scratch the felt surface of the table behind his cards with his index finger, and this is also a signal for a hit. Either signal is universally accepted in American casinos.

If that same player wants to stand with his total, he simply waves his hand over the cards, with the palm face down, and the dealer will respect this signal and pass him by.

24

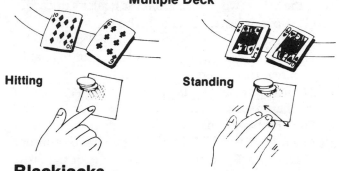

Multiple Deck

Hitting

Standing

Blackjacks

If a player is fortunate enough to be dealt a black-jack, which is an ace and 10-value card dealt to him as an original hand, he also turns these over immediately. But now for the good news. If the dealer doesn't have a blackjack also, the player will be paid off at once at 3-2, and his cards will be taken out of play.

Dealer's Upcard

In single deck games, if the dealer's upcard is a 10 (or 10-value), he immediately peeks at his hole card (the face down card below the upcard) to see if he has a blackjack. If he does, he turns the ace over and collects bets from all players who themselves don't have blackjacks. If he doesn't have an ace in the hole, he continues dealing the game.

If the dealer has an ace as an upcard, then he will ask the players if they want *insurance*. We'll go into this later.

Playing the Hand

Let's assume, in our theoretical game at the table

25

with the other two players, that the dealer's upcard is a 9. He doesn't have to peek at his hole card, for there's no way he can have a blackjack with a 9 showing.

The first baseman is the first to act on his hand. Remember, the players act first—that is, hit or stand—and then the dealer acts last, after all the players have made their decisions.

The first baseman scrapes his cards for a hit. He is dealt a queen. He scrapes the cards again for another hit, and gets a 7. Disgustedly, he turns over the cards he has been holding. He had a 3 and a 2, making his original hand a 5; with the queen and 7 he now holds 22, and has busted. The dealer takes away the first baseman's chips and cards and now turns his attention to the second player.

This player scrapes for a hit, gets a 4, and then happily slides his cards under his chips, a signal that he is now standing on his total. The dealer now turns to us. We look at our cards and find we hold a jack and a 9. Our 19 is a strong total, so we stand by—sliding the cards under our chips. Now it's the dealer's turn. He turns over his hole card.

His hole card was a 3, giving him a total of 12. Under the rules of the game, he must hit this hand, since it totals less than 17. He takes a card for himself by putting the top card of the stock face up next to his two original cards. It is a 4, giving him a 16. He must hit again. He has no options. His next card is a king. The dealer has gone over 21 and busted.

At this point, he takes the second player's original cards from under the chips and turns them over. This player had a 10 and a 6 for a 16, and drew the 4, giving him a 20. He is paid off at even-money. We are also paid off at even-money. It really didn't matter what totals either we or the second baseman had at this point, since the dealer busted and automatically lost.

After all the discards are put away, another round of play begins. Again, we all get two cards, and the dealer's upcard this time is a jack. Therefore, he peeks at his hole card, and when he finds he doesn't have a blackjack, he now turns toward the first baseman and the game goes on as before.

After a few rounds of play, even though there are cards left in the stock the dealer is holding, he'll shuffle up the cards. This is done to prevent card counters, experts who keep track of played out cards, from having an advantage over the house by knowing just what cards are left in the stock and betting accordingly.

Multiple Deck Games

By multiple deck games, we are referring to all games which use more than one deck.

When 4 or more decks are used, they're dealt from a **shoe**, a rectangular box which permits the cards to be slid out one at a time.

Double Deck Games

When two decks are used, these are still hand-held and all signals used by players are the same as in a single deck game. There are relatively few double deck games in comparison with either single or four and six deck games.

Splitting Pairs

Doubling Down

V. The Player's Options

Splitting Pairs

A player may split any matching cards of the same rank (pairs) if dealt as an original hand. For example, if he or she is dealt two 8s, these may be split. When pairs are split, they are turned over by the player if dealt face down; or separated, if dealt face up. Then a bet equal to the original bet is placed on the newly split card.

For example, if a player had bet $5, and received two 8s, and split them, then an additional $5 bet will be placed on the separated (split) 8. In essence, the player will now be betting on and playing out two hands.

He draws cards on the first 8 till he is satisfied with that total, and then he draws cards to the second 8, just as though this was an original hand.

Any pairs can be split, and for purposes of pairs, all 10-value cards are considered pairs. For example, a 10 and queen, or a jack and king, are considered pairs, but as we shall see, 10s should not be split.

Aces may be split, but unlike all other pairs, only one additional card will be dealt to each ace. Nevertheless, aces equal 11 and they should always be split.

Doubling Down

A player may double his bet on his original hand, at his option. When he does this, he will receive an additional card, and *one card* only. Therefore, it's important to remember that after doubling down, you can't stand on your original hand's total; you're going to be given an additional card by the dealer.

In practically all casinos except for the Northern Nevada ones, the rules permit doubling down on any two-card total. In Northern Nevada, only 10s and 11s may be doubled down.

When doubling down, a player turns over his cards if dealt face down, and puts out a bet equal to the original bet. When the cards have been dealt face up, he simply puts out an additional bet.

Surrender

In a few casinos, the player is allowed to forfeit half his original bet if he or she doesn't want to play the hand against the dealer. This is called **surrender.**

For example, suppose a player has a big bet out and the dealer shows a 10 as his upcard. The player has been dealt a 16, and feels that if he hits the hand, he'll bust, and if he stands, the dealer will have a 17 or more to beat him anyway. So, in those casinos allowing surrender, this player may surrender his hand. It's one of the few instances in which a verbal statement of the player's intent is made. He says *"Surrender,"* and the dealer will remove his cards and half his bet.

Insurance

When the dealer's upcard is an ace, before he peeks at his hole card the players are given the opportunity to *insure* their bets. The dealer will ask "Insurance?" and the players may bet up to one-half of their original bet that the dealer has a 10-value card in the hole.

If the dealer has a blackjack, the insurance bet wins, and is paid off at 2-1, but the original bet loses, and so, in essence, it's a standoff.

Therefore, an insurance bet is really a wager that the dealer has a blackjack. If he has one, the bet wins. If he doesn't have a 10-value card in the hole, the insurance bet is immediately lost and taken away and the game continues.

For example, if a player had a $10 bet out and then made a $5 insurance bet and the dealer didn't have a blackjack, the $5 bet would be taken away by the dealer. However, the game would now continue and the original $10 bet is still valid.

If the dealer in the above instance had a blackjack, he'd take away the player's original $10 bet and then pay $10, at 2-1 on the $5 insurance bet. In essence, it's a push.

VI. Winning Basic Strategies

Now we come to the chapter that will show you how to win at blackjack, using correct basic strategies.

Hitting and Standing Strategy

We'll divide this strategy into hard and soft totals. Remember, a hard hand is anyone that doesn't contain an ace, or where an ace is counted as a 1 and not an 11.

For our considerations, all hard hands will begin with a total of 12. Hands below that total can be hit without worrying about busting.

Whether to hit or stand on any hand depends on two factors: the player's total and the dealer's upcard.

The following table will show the correct hitting and standing basic strategies:

Chart 1
Hitting and Standing—Hard Totals

	2	3	4	5	6	7	8	9	10	A
11 or less	H	H	H	H	H	H	H	H	H	H
12	H	H	S	S	S	H	H	H	H	H
13	S	S	S	S	S	H	H	H	H	H
14	S	S	S	S	S	H	H	H	H	H
15	S	S	S	S	S	H	H	H	H	H
16	S	S	S	S	S	H	H	H	H	H
17-21	S	S	S	S	S	S	S	S	S	S

H = Hit   S = Stand

Whenever the dealer shows a 7 or higher upcard (8, 9, 10 or ace), we assume that he already has a total of 17 and must stand with that total. Of course, that's not always the case, but it happens frequently enough for us to try and improve our total if it's below 17.

That's why we hit all hands from 12 through 16 when the dealer shows a 7, 8, 9, 10 or ace.

When the dealer shows a *bust* or *stiff* card, a 2, 3, 4, 5, or 6, we stand on all totals, except a hard 12 against a dealer's 2 or 3.

The reason we hit a 12 against a dealer's 2 or 3 up-card is that there are relatively fewer cards to bust our (and the dealer's) hand in that situation. Other than a 12 against the 2 and 3, we stand on all other totals when the dealer shows a stiff card. Our strategy in this regard is to force the dealer to hit his stiff hand and bust it, while we still have a valid hand.

It may be hard to memorize the table, but if you play out and practice some hands at home looking at the hitting and standing table, it will become easier to understand. And if you see the reasoning behind it, it's easier still.

Of course, we never hit a hard 17 or higher total, no matter what the dealer shows. The odds are very strong that we'll bust, and if our total is 19 or better we're favored to win by standing.

What we don't want to do is hit stiff totals from 12 to 16 when the dealer shows a 4, 5 or 6. These are the worst cards the dealer can have (and the best for us to see as upcards) because he's most likely to bust his hand with those upcards. And it would be foolish of us to bust first, when the dealer has such a good chance of busting and losing.

Hitting and Standing with Soft Totals

A soft total is any hand that contains an ace which is counted as 11 points. Thus, an ace-6 is a soft 17. There will be two tables here—the first is to be used in all jurisdictions other than Northern Nevada, for only hard 10s and 11s can be doubled down there.

Chart 2
Hitting, Standing or Doubling Down with Soft Totals

	2	3	4	5	6	7	8	9	10	A
A2-A5	H	H	D	D	D	H	H	H	H	H
A6	D	D	D	D	D	H	H	H	H	H
A7	S	D	D	D	D	S	S	H	H	S
A8	S	S	S	S	S	S	S	S	S	S
A9	S	S	S	S	S	S	S	S	S	S

H = Hit   S = Stand   D = Double

All soft totals of 17 or below should be hit or doubled down. When the dealer shows a 4, 5 or 6 these soft totals will be doubled down.

The ace-6, the soft 17, will *never be stood upon.* It will either be hit, or doubled down. When you see a player standing with a soft 17, you'll know he's very weak, and a loser.

The soft 19 and 20 are very strong and you should be content to stand with these totals. But the soft 18 is the tricky one. It is hit against the dealer's 9 and 10 up-card, and doubled down when the dealer holds the 3 through the 6. Practice these hands, and it will come naturally to you after a while.

The next table is for use only in Northern Nevada or any other jurisdiction where soft doubling down is not permitted.

Chart 3
Hitting and Standing with Soft Totals

	2	3	4	5	6	7	8	9	10	A
A2-A6	H	H	H	H	H	H	H	H	H	H
A7	S	S	S	S	S	S	S	H	H	S
A8-A9	S	S	S	S	S	S	S	S	S	S

H = Hit   S = Stand

As we see from the above table, we *always hit* the soft 17, and hit the soft 18 against the dealer's 9 or 10. These are important rules to remember, as well as standing on soft 19 or 20.

Doubling Down Strategies

The next table shows doubling down strategies, which correctly followed, give the player a tremendous edge over the casino. This table covers only hard doubling down totals, since the soft ones have already been covered in the previous section.

In Northern Nevada, where only a hard 10 or 11 can be doubled down, use the lines showing the 10 and 11.

Chart 4
Doubling Down with Hard Totals

	2	3	4	5	6	7	8	9	10	A
8(5-3,4-4)				D	D					
9		D	D	D	D					
10	D	D	D	D	D	D	D	D		
11	D	D	D	D	D	D	D	D	D	D

D = Double Down   Blank = Do Not Double Down

From this table we see that we *never* double down with a hard total of less than 8. Be sure to double down when you hold an 11. Many players are afraid to double down against a dealer's 10, but if you get a 10-value card on the 11, you have a 21, and can't lose.

If playing in Atlantic City, or in a casino where the dealer doesn't look at his hole card till all the players have acted upon their hands, the same double down rules apply. If the dealer finds he has a blackjack, the extra double down wager will be returned. The same holds true when splitting pairs. Only the original bet is lost.

Splitting Pairs

As we know, a player has the option of splitting any paired cards from his original hand, such as 3-3, 8-8, 9-9 and so forth. And all 10-value cards are considered pairs, such as jack-king, or 10-queen. The following chart shows correct splitting strategies. Split only those pairs shown on the chart.

36

Be sure to split 8s and aces. A pair of 8s add up to 16, the worst stiff total a player can have, while 8s separately will form the base for a much stronger hand.

And aces should be split, because each ace adds up to 11, and a 10-value card drawn to that 11 is a powerful 21.

On the other hand, never split 4s and 5s. Two 4s add up to 8, while an individual 4 can end up as a stiff hand and a bad one at that. The 5s together add up to 10, and in most situations will be a doubled down hand. An individual 5 will usually lead to a stiff or a busted hand.

Don't split 10s (any 10-value pairs). These add up to 20, usually a winning hand. Splitting 10s is a bad move, and only the weakest players make it.

Some players will split any pair, no matter what the

dealer's upcard, thinking this is correct. But it isn't, and will end up costing the player money. Stick to our pair splits and you'll come out a winner. They all make sense.

For example, we don't split 7s against an 8 because if the player gets two 10-value cards, one on each 7, he'll still have only 17 and the dealer might already have an 18. And we don't split 9s against a dealer's 7 because two 9s add up to an 18, and the dealer might only have a 17. And we split 9s against the 8 because the 18 might only be a push, whereas a 10-value card on a 9 makes it a winner.

Resplitting Pairs

If an original pair should be split, then subsequent cards of the same rank should also be split. For example, suppose the dealer shows a 6 as his upcard, and you have a pair of 8s. You split the 8s, and get a 5 on the first 8 for a 13. Now you must stand on that hand because the *Hitting and Standing Strategies* call for no further cards to be drawn.

On the second 8, you're dealt another 8. This should be split and another bet put out. The rule is: resplit pairs where the first split is correct. Not all casinos allow resplitting. For example, aces generally can't be resplit. All other pairs can be re-split in practically all casinos except in Atlantic City.

Insurance

Whenever the dealer shows an ace as his upcard, he'll ask if any player wants insurance. As explained before, the insurance bet is a bet that the dealer **has** a

10-value card in the hole and thus has a blackjack.

In most cases, it's a bad bet. Don't take insurance unless you're familiar with an advanced card counting system.

Surrender

This is allowed in some casinos, where a player may forfeit half his bet and decide not to play his or her original hand against the dealer.

When you have the chance to surrender, stick to the following rules: surrender 15s and 16s against a dealer's 10, and a 16 against a dealer's ace. (Do not surrender 8-8—split it.)

Otherwise, don't surrender.

Chart 6
Master Strategy Chart

	2	3	4	5	6	7	8	9	10	A
7 or less	H	H	H	H	H	H	H	H	H	H
62	H	H	H	H	H	H	H	H	H	H
44, 53	H	H	H	D	D	H	H	H	H	H
9	D	D	D	D	D	H	H	H	H	H
10	D	D	D	D	D	D	D	D	H	H
11	D	D	D	D	D	D	D	D	D	D
12	H	H	S	S	S	H	H	H	H	H
13	S	S	S	S	S	H	H	H	H	H
14	S	S	S	S	S	H	H	H	H	H
15	S	S	S	S	S	H	H	H	H	H
16	S	S	S	S	S	H	H	H	H	H
A2	H	H	D*	D*	D*	H	H	H	H	H
A3	H	H	D*	D*	D*	H	H	H	H	H
A4	H	H	D*	D*	D*	H	H	H	H	H
A5	H	H	D*	D*	D*	H	H	H	H	H
A6	D*	D*	D*	D*	D*	H	H	H	H	H
A7	S	D*	D*	D*	D*	S	S	H	H	S
A8	S	S	S	S	S	S	S	S	S	S
A9	S	S	S	S	S	S	S	S	S	S
22	H	Spl.	Spl.	Spl.	Spl.	Spl.	H	H	H	H
33	H	H	Spl.	Spl.	Spl.	Spl.	H	H	H	H
66	Spl.	Spl.	Spl.	Spl.	Spl.	H	H	H	H	H
77	Spl.	Spl.	Spl.	Spl.	Spl.	Spl.	H	H	H	H
88	Spl.	Spl.	Spl.	Spl.	Spl.	Spl.	Spl.	Spl.	Spl.	Spl.
99	Spl.	Spl.	Spl.	Spl.	Spl.	S	Spl.	Spl.	S	S
AA	Spl.	Spl.	Spl.	Spl.	Spl.	Spl.	Spl.	Spl.	Spl.	Spl.

H = Hit   S = Stand   D = Double   Spl. = Split

*Where soft doubling not permitted, as in Northern Nevada, hit (do not double).

VII. Card Counting and Money Management

Card Counting

Card counting, or keeping track of the cards already played out, is used by experts to beat the casino, and many of these experts have been barred from play.

This guidebook is not going to deal with card counting, other than to state that when a high proportion of 10-value cards and aces have been dealt out, the deck is unfavorable for the player. On the other hand, many smaller cards, such as 2s, 3s, 4s, 5s, 6s and 7s have been dealt out, the deck or decks are favorable for the player.

By watching the game closely, a player can get a good idea of the cards already dealt. For example, if on the first round of play in a single deck game, a disproportionate number of aces and 10s were dealt, then the deck is unfavorable. If a whole group of smaller cards showed on the opening round, with few aces or tens, then the deck is favorable.

A good rule in a single deck game only is to raise the bet when the first round showed a high proportion of small cards dealt out, and to lower the bet when this round showed a higher proportion of tens and aces.

With each round that follows, you see that cumulatively, more tens than normal have been dealt, keep your bet low. On the other hand, when you notice more small cards have been played out, raise your bet. This strategy works because a single deck is sensitive to changes in deck composition.

To effectively beat the casinos, whether playing a single or multiple deck game, we highly recommend that you learn a card counting strategy.

See back page for information on the GRI Pro-Count; the most effective card counting strategy ever produced for the average player. It is simple to learn yet extremely powerful. It will give any reader of this book a winning edge over the casino with just a few hours practice at home.

Money Management

Blackjack games can be like rollercoasters, with large winning and losing swings during the course of play. Be prepared and don't get discouraged by these swings, because correct play will make you a winner in the long run.

As a rule of thumb, multiply your normal bet by 40 to determine how much to put on the table for one session of play. If you're betting $2 at a time, $80 will be sufficient. With $5 bets, about $200 will be needed. You can even hedge and take less, about $50 for $2 bets and $100 for $5 bets, but that's cutting it a little too thin.

Remember, play only with money you can afford to lose, that won't affect you financially and/or emotionally. Try to double your stake at the table. If you do, leave at once. You've done well. Or, if the table is choppy, and you're ahead, endeavor to leave a winner.

If you're losing, don't lose more than you bring to the table. Set a loss limit, and never reach into your pocket for more money. The first loss is the cheapest.

Money management can be as important as good play. Keep control of your emotions and your money, and you'll be a winner.

VIII. Glossary of Blackjack Terms

Anchorman—Also called **Third Baseman.** The player in the last seat or the player who acts upon his hand last at the table.

Blackjack—1. The name of the casino game; also known as "21." 2. An original hand consisting of an ace and 10-value card, paid off at 3-2 if held by a player.

Burning a Card—The removal of the top card by the dealer before dealing out cards on the first round of play.

Busting—Also known as **Breaking.** Drawing cards to a hand so that its total is 22 or more, a loser.

Card Counting—Keeping mental track of the cards played out to see if the deck is favorable or unfavorable.

Chips—The gambling tokens issued by the casino to take the place of cash, for betting purposes.

Dealer—The casino employee in charge of the blackjack game, who deals out cards and collects and pays off bets.

Deck—The standard pack of cards containing 52 cards of four suits.

Double Down—The doubling of an original bet by a player, who will then receive only one additional card.

Draw—See **Hit**.

Favorable Deck—A deck whose remaining cards are to the advantage of the player as far as probability of winning is concerned.

First Baseman—The player who receives cards and acts upon them first. Usually occupies the first end seat at the table.

Hand—The cards the players hold and act upon.

Hard Total—A hand containing no aces, or where the ace is counted as 1.

Hit—Also called **Draw**. The act of getting one or more cards for the original hand.

Hole Card—The unseen dealer's card.

Insurance—A bet that can be made when a dealer shows an ace as an upcard. This bet wins if the dealer has a blackjack.

Multiple Deck—The use of more than one deck in the game of casino blackjack.

Natural—A term for a blackjack.

Push—A tie between the dealer and player, where no money changes hands. It's a standoff.

Round of Play—A complete cycle of play where all the players and the dealer act upon their hands.

Shoe—A device used when dealing four or more decks.

Shuffle, Shuffle Up—The mixing up of the cards by the dealer.

Single Deck Game—A game in which only one deck of cards is used.

Soft Total—A hand containing an ace that counts as 11 points. Example, an ace-9 is a soft 20 total.

Splitting Pairs—The separation of two cards of equal rank, such as 8s, so that they're played as two separate hands.

Standing, Standing Pat—Not hitting a hand.

Stiff Hand—Any hand that may bust if drawn to, such as a hard 12-16.

Ten-Value Card—The 10, jack, queen or king, all valued at ten points.

Third Baseman—See **Anchorman**.

Tip or Toke—A gratuity given to or bet for the dealer by a player.

Twenty-One—Another name for the casino game of blackjack.

Upcard—The open card of the dealer which can be seen by the players prior to their acting on their hands.

GRI Master Lesson
Strategy & Tactic Plans
—Exclusive Offer—

Now, after years of underground use, and for the **first time**, Gambling Research Institute has released the GRI Master Lesson, Strategy & Tactic Plans to the general public—and at substantial savings!

This 10,000 word strategy bonanza, **previously unreleased**, contains the all **new**, latest and up-to-date **improved** strategies and casino savvy techniques developed by the GRI Research teams. Much of this information can be found only here, sweated out by our professional affiliates in casinos around the world.

MASTER BLACKJACK

Learn what it takes to be a **master player.** Be a **powerhouse** looked on with envy by lesser players. Learn with just a little effort to make average winning sessions into **blockbusters** and, conversely, when and how to cut losses. The GRI papers cover everything from the psychological and emotional aspects of blackjack to the ten-factor, the Ace-factor, the effects of rules variations, single and multiple deck games, the **true count** and much, much more.

And, of course, you'll receive the GRI Pro-Count.

BONUS & EXTRA BONUS!

Not only will we give you the "GRI Pro-Count Guide: How to Disguise the Fact that You're an Expert" ($15 value), but you'll also receive the GRI Research Team's "Professional Money Managment Guide"!

To Order, send ~~$249⁹⁵~~ $149⁹⁵ by bank check or money order to:

GRI
P.O. Box 5267
Santa Cruz, CA 95063

SAVE $100⁰⁰

Take 40% Off! Regular ~~$249⁹⁵~~ - Only $149⁹⁵ with coupon

Yes! I want to take advantage of this **special offer!** Please **rush** me the GRI Pro-Count Master Lesson Plan. Enclosed is a check or money order payable to GRI for $149⁹⁵ I understand that the GRI Pro-Count guide, "How to Disguise the Fact that You're an Expert" **and** the "Professional Money Management Guide" (each a $15 Value) **will still be included free!**

Name _____

Address_____

City_____ State_____ Zip_____
